Science and Social Studies

Interactive Skills Handbook

Grade 2

 SRA

Columbus, OH

SRAonline.com

 SRA

When Can You Use It?

You can use this handbook any time. It can help you read for information as you read

- a textbook,
- an encyclopedia article, or
- a magazine.

How Is It Organized?

The lessons in this handbook focus on

📖 **Features**   text features, such as headings and charts.

📑 **Structures**   text structures, such as sequence.

✔ **Skills**   comprehension skills, such as predicting and summarizing.

Each lesson has four parts:

1. **Learn It** tells you about the topic.
2. **Try It** helps you check your understanding.
3. **Practice It** provides practice exercises.
4. **Apply It** provides exercises that challenge you to apply what you've learned about the topic.

Bonus Feature! ....

Look at the graphic organizers on pages 106–111. Use them to take notes as you read. Or make your own on a separate piece of paper. They help you organize and understand information.

Table of Contents

Text Features

Text Structures

Comprehension Skills

Graphic Organizers

Learn It

When you read, look for words in boldface type.

A word in **boldface type** is darker and thicker than other words around it. Boldface type is used to get your attention. The following kinds of words may be printed in boldface type:

- **vocabulary words**
- **headings and subheadings**

> This heading tells what the paragraph is about.

Digging a Well

   Wells are used to store water. A well must be very deep. It takes a long time to dig a deep hole in the ground. When the shovel hits **bedrock,** it is time to stop. There is no way a shovel can break up the hard rock!

> This vocabulary word is in boldface type.

 Rule to Remember **Pay extra attention to words in boldface type.**

Interactive Skills Handbook • Grade 2

Try It

Use what you know about words in boldface type to answer the questions below.

> **We Need Oxygen**
>
>   Did you know that we need trees and other plants to live? Trees and plants help make the **oxygen** that we breathe. Trees and plants take in water and **carbon dioxide,** and they make oxygen. We cannot live without oxygen.

1. What is the heading of the paragraph?

   _____

2. Which words are two new vocabulary words in the paragraph?

   _____

3. How can you tell which words are new vocabulary words?

   _____

Practice It

Use the passage and the picture to answer the questions below.

The New Food Pyramid

The new food **pyramid** has six colored stripes. Each stripe stands for a food group. You should eat healthful foods from each food group every day.

| Grains | Vegetables | Fruits | Milk | Meat & Beans |

Oils Oils are not a food group but you need some for good health.

U.S. Department of Agriculture

4. Why is the word *pyramid* in boldface type?

_____

5. Why is the phrase *The New Food Pyramid* in boldface type?

_____

Apply It

Choose one of the topics below. Write a heading and three or four sentences about that topic. Use at least two of the vocabulary words given.

Planting a Seed: seed, water, soil, roots

Swimming at a Pool: lifeguard, safety, dive

6. My heading: _____

7. My sentences:

_____

_____

_____

_____

_____

_____

_____

Learn It

Charts make information easier to understand. There are different kinds of charts.

- An **organizational chart** groups things.

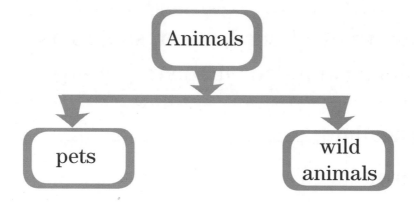

- A **T-chart** compares two things.

Apples and Bananas

Apple	Banana
An apple is a fruit.	A banana is a fruit.
An apple is round.	A banana is long.

 Pay attention to charts and the information they show.

Try It

Use this chart of the seasons to answer the questions below.

Seasons

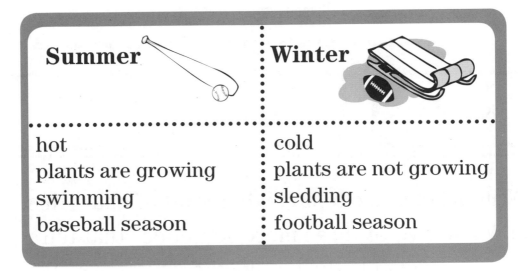

Summer	Winter
hot	cold
plants are growing	plants are not growing
swimming	sledding
baseball season	football season

1. What is the name of this chart?

_____

2. Which season is good for sledding?

_____

3. What kind of chart is this?

  a. organizational chart

  b. T-chart

Practice It

Fill in the blanks in the chart below.

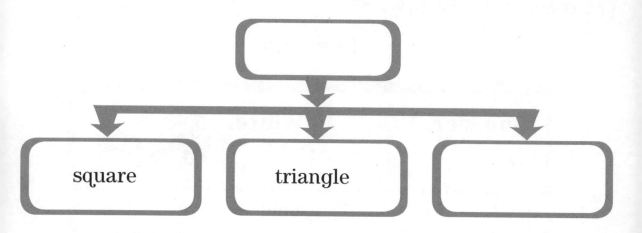

Write a sentence telling what kind of chart this is. Write two or three more sentences that tell why you filled in the blanks the way you did.

_____

_____

_____

_____

_____

_____

Apply It

Use this chart to compare dogs and cats. Write a title for the chart on the line. Write details about each animal below its name.

Title: _____

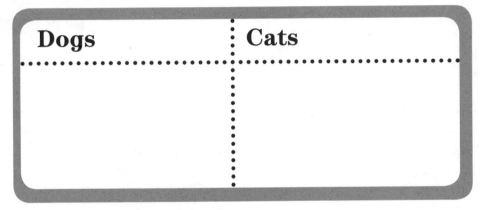

Dogs	Cats

Write two or three sentences describing the chart.

_____

_____

_____

Learn It

A diagram is a drawing that shows parts of something or the way something works.

This diagram shows how a dandelion grows.

Life of a Dandelion

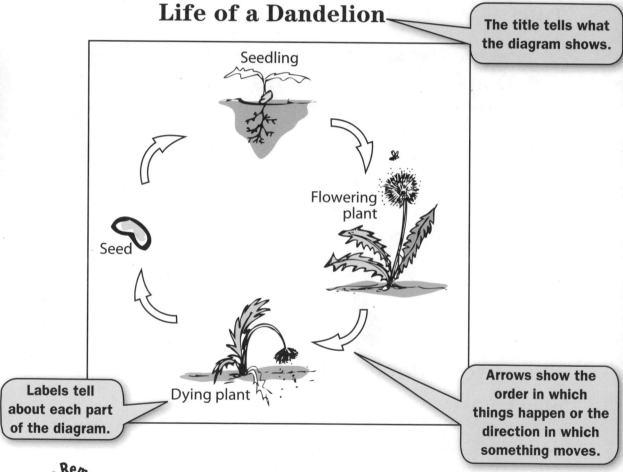

The title tells what the diagram shows.

Seedling

Flowering plant

Seed

Dying plant

Labels tell about each part of the diagram.

Arrows show the order in which things happen or the direction in which something moves.

 Read the title, labels, and arrows on a diagram to understand what is being shown.

Try It

Look at the diagram below. Then answer the questions.

Parts of a Bicycle

seat

handle

hand brakes

spokes

tires

chain　pedals

1. What is the name of this diagram?

_____

2. What are two of the labels in this diagram?

_____

_____

3. Where do you sit on this bicycle?

_____

Practice It

Use the diagram to answer the questions below.

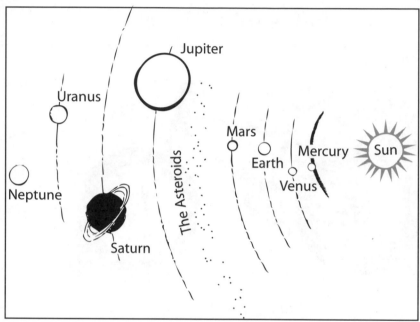

4. Which planet is closest to the sun?

_____

5. Which planet has rings around it?

_____

6. Where is Earth in relation to the sun?

_____

7. Which two planets is Earth between?

_____

Apply It

Complete the passage by writing things about yourself. Draw and label a diagram to show what the passage says.

All About Me

My name is _____. I am

_____ years old. I have _____

arms and _____ legs. I have

_____ ears and _____ nose.

My eyes are _____, and I have a

_____ smile.

Learn It

A glossary is a list of vocabulary words and their meanings.

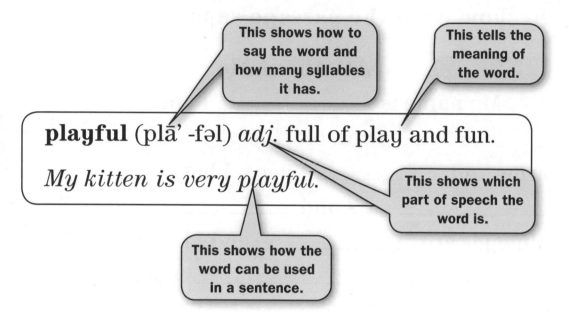

This shows how to say the word and how many syllables it has.

This tells the meaning of the word.

playful (plā' -fəl) *adj.* full of play and fun.

My kitten is very playful.

This shows which part of speech the word is.

This shows how the word can be used in a sentence.

 Use the glossary to find information about vocabulary words.

Try It

Use what you know about glossaries to answer the questions below.

> **display** (di splā') *v.* to show.
> *She wanted to display the flag.*
>
> **principal** (prin' sə pəl) *n.* the person in charge of a school.
> *Ms. Lin is the principal of the school.*

1. What part of speech is the word *display*?

   a. noun   **b.** verb   **c.** adjective

2. How many syllables does the word *principal* have?

   a. one   **b.** two   **c.** three

3. What does *display* mean?

   a. the person in charge of a school

   b. to show

   c. full of play and fun

Practice It

Write the words from the glossary on the correct lines in the passage below.

> **settlers** (set' lərs) *n.* people who move to a new part of the country.
> *The settlers faced many hardships.*
>
> **sod** (sod) *n.* the grass-covered surface of the ground.
> *Sod is often laid around new houses.*

Sod Houses

When the _____ moved west, they used grass to build houses. Many settlers moved to the prairie where there were no trees to build houses with. The settlers cut squares of _____ from the ground. They used the sod to make the walls and roofs of their houses. The floors in most of the houses were just dirt.

Apply It

Number the glossary entries below to put them in alphabetical order. Then write a sentence for each entry. Underline the glossary word in your sentence.

___ **house** (hous) *n.* a building that a family can live in

_____

___ **drowsy** (drau' zē) *adj.* ready to fall asleep

_____

___ **imagine** (i ma' jən) *v.* to make a picture in your mind

_____

 Features

Learn It

Headings help you find the main idea of a paragraph or passage.

A **heading** is the title of a section of writing. Headings describe what you will read in that section of the writing.

Acoma: Sky City

This is the heading.

    Acoma is a very old city. It was built on a tall, flat mesa in New Mexico. The city is known as Sky City because it seems to be so close to the sky. The city was built on the mesa to keep it safe. The houses in Acoma are made of dried clay. They stand about three stories high.

The sentences in this paragraph tell about the heading.

 Rule to Remember **Headings tell you what a paragraph or passage is about. There can be more than one heading on a page.**

Try It

Choose the best heading for each paragraph. One heading will not be used.

> **Longhouses   Tepees   Adobe Homes**

1. _____

Long ago, many Native Americans lived in deserts. They built adobe homes. They used dried mud, straw, and clay to build their homes. Rooms could be added to the tops of adobe homes.

2. _____

Some Native Americans lived in forests. They built longhouses. Longhouses had wooden frames. The walls were covered with bark. Inside was a long hallway. There were rooms on each side of the hallway.

Practice It

Choose the best heading for each passage.

American Soils

Cloud Types

Reading Food Labels

3. You want to learn about the kinds of soil in America. You should read the paragraph with the heading

_____.

4. You want to learn about which vitamins are in your food. You should read the paragraph with the heading

_____.

5. You want to learn about the things you see in the sky and the weather they bring. You should read the paragraph with the heading

_____.

Apply It

Read the paragraphs below. The first one has a heading. Write a heading for the other paragraph.

George Washington Carver

George Washington Carver was born around 1861 in Missouri. He lived on a farm. He liked to paint pictures of plants and flowers.

6. _____

Carver told farmers to plant peanuts. The peanuts would help the soil and provide good food to eat. But many people did not want to buy peanuts. So Carver made a list of 300 things that could be made using peanuts. Then many people bought and used peanuts.

Learn It

A numbered list shows the order of steps needed to do something.

The list below shows the order of steps needed to make a tomato sandwich.

How to Make a Tomato Sandwich

1. Ask an adult to cut a tomato into slices.

2. Put the slices on one piece of bread.

3. Spread mustard on another piece of bread.

4. Put the pieces of bread together and enjoy!

 A numbered list shows the order of steps needed to do something.

Try It

The steps needed to wash a bike are shown below, but they are out of order. Write a number next to each step to show the correct order.

_____ Scrub the bike with soapy water.

_____ Put a little soap in the water.

_____ Fill a bucket with water.

_____ Spray the bike with a hose to wash off the soapy water.

Practice It

Under each picture, write a number to show the correct order of the steps for feeding a dog.

_____

_____

_____

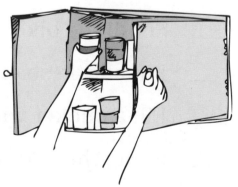

_____

Apply It

Think of something you do every day. Write the steps you take in the correct order. Add a title to the top of your list.

Title: _____

1. _____

   _____

2. _____

   _____

3. _____

   _____

4. _____

   _____

5. _____

   _____

Learn It

A photo helps readers understand a story. A caption is the words or sentences that tell about the photo.

In the late 1800s, Sitting Bull was the brave leader of thousands of Native Americans.

This photo is from a story about Sitting Bull. It shows what Sitting Bull looked like. The caption gives information about the photo. The caption tells the name of the man and when he lived. It also tells a little about who he was.

 Look at photos and read captions to learn more information about what you are reading.

Try It

Draw a line from each caption to the photo it tells about.

Blue poison dart frogs are not very good swimmers.

Sunflower seeds are a healthful snack for people and birds.

A queen honeybee can lay more than 1,500 eggs in one day.

Practice It

Use what you know about photos and captions to answer the question below.

Ellen Ochoa was the world's first Hispanic female astronaut. She has been to space four times.

Who is Ellen Ochoa?

_____

_____

_____

_____

Apply It

Pretend that this is a picture of your school. Write a caption for the picture. Include details about your school in your caption.

Caption:

_____

_____

_____

_____

_____

Learn It

A symbol is something that represents or stands for something else. Government symbols are things that stand for the United States and its government.

The American flag stands for our country and our government.

The American bald eagle represents strength and the freedom we have in the United States.

The Statue of Liberty symbolizes freedom around the world.

 Rule to Remember Government symbols are things that represent our country or government.

Try It

Read the passage below. Then answer the questions.

Symbol of America

The Liberty Bell was rung in 1776 to celebrate the United States becoming a free country. Now it is a symbol of freedom in the United States. The Liberty Bell is in a museum in Philadelphia.

1. Why was the Liberty Bell rung in 1776?

_____

_____

2. Where is the Liberty Bell now?

_____

_____

Practice It

Draw a line from each symbol to the correct information.

The U.S. flag is red, white, and blue. It has 13 stripes and 50 stars.

The Statue of Liberty holds a torch. It is 151 feet tall and is in New York Harbor.

The Liberty Bell was made in 1752. It cracked the first time it was rung.

Interactive Skills Handbook • Grade 2

Apply It

Write a sentence telling what each symbol stands for.

3. _____
_____
_____
_____

4. _____
_____
_____
_____

5. _____
_____
_____
_____

Learn It

A table of contents tells you where to find information in a book.

A **table of contents** is at the beginning of a book. It gives the title and page number of each important part of the book.

The Solar System Table of Contents	Page
Stars	3
Planets	7
Meteors	15
Glossary	21

This table of contents is from a book about the solar system. It gives the name and page number of each section in the book. If you wanted to read about planets, you would have to turn to page 7 in this book.

 Use a table of contents to find important information in a book.

Interactive Skills Handbook • Grade 2

Try It

Use the table of contents to answer the questions below.

All About Sally Ride

Table of Contents	Page
Meet Sally Ride	3
Sally Ride Goes to Space	8
Sally Ride the Teacher	15

1. If you want to read about Sally Ride going to space, which page should you turn to?

   a. 3

   b. 8

2. Which section is not in this table of contents?

   a. Sally Ride Goes to School

   b. Meet Sally Ride

Practice It

The table of contents below is missing some information. Choose the correct words or numbers from the box to fill in the blanks.

15   City of Clownfish   3

Fish Tales

Table of Contents	**Page**
Chapter 1: The Catfish Caper	__
Chapter 2: _____	9
Chapter 3: Goldfish Nuggets	__

Use the table of contents above to answer the question.

3. On which page does Chapter 2 begin?

    a. 7

    b. 9

Apply It

Pretend you are writing a book about a week in your life. Fill in the blanks to complete your table of contents.

Title: _____

Table of _____   ____

Chapter 1: Starting My Day   2

Chapter 2: _____   4

_____

Chapter 3: The End of the Day   8

Chapter 4: It's the Weekend!   10

Choose two chapters. Write a sentence for each chapter that tells what kind of information a reader would find on those pages.

_____

_____

_____

_____

Learn It

Tables organize information about a topic.
A **table** organizes information in rows and columns. To understand a table, read the title first. Next, read the headings. Finally, read the information in each row.

> Read the information in each row from left to right.

> The title tells what the table is about.

> The headings tell what kind of information is in each column.

Playing Games

Game	Number of Players	Indoor or Outdoor
Hopscotch	2 or more	Outdoor
Musical Chairs	3 or more	Indoor
Tag	2 or more	Outdoor
Go Fish	2 or more	Indoor

Rule to Remember

Read the title and headings to understand information in a table.

Try It

Use the table below to answer the questions.

Common Fruits

Fruit	Taste	Color	Grows on Trees?
apple	sweet	red	yes
plum	sweet	purple	yes
lemon	sour	yellow	yes
orange	sweet	orange	yes
strawberry	sweet	red	no
banana	swect	yellow	yes

1. Are strawberries sweet or sour?

_____

2. What color are plums?

_____

3. Which red fruit grows on trees?

_____

4. Which fruit is yellow and sour?

_____

Practice It

Read the chart below about inventions.
Then answer the questions.

Great Inventions for Kids

Invention	Inventor	Year Invented	State Where Invented
bubble gum	Walter Diemer	1928	Pennsylvania
blue jeans	Levi Strauss	1873	California
chocolate chip cookies	Ruth Wakefield	1930	Massachusetts
crayons	Edwin Binney and Harold Smith	1903	New York

5. Who invented crayons?

_____

6. What did Levi Strauss invent?

_____

Apply It

Complete the table to give information about the objects in your classroom. Give your table a title. Include information about the windows, tables, desks, chairs, and other objects in your classroom.

Title: _____

Objects	How many?	What color?
doors		
windows		
tables		
desks		
chairs		

Learn It

Understanding cause and effect can help you read.

- The **cause** is why something happens.
- The **effect** is what happens.

> The bag ripped. → The egg broke. The milk spilled.

Cause-and-Effect Signal Words		
because	:	makes
when	:	that is why
so	:	so that
which	:	if . . . then

Ask yourself what happens and why as you read.

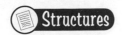

Try It

Draw a line from each cause to its effect.

Cause	Effect
1. It makes me feel better	it makes me happy.
2. When she tells a funny joke,	we laugh.
3. When someone asks me to join a game,	to eat right and exercise.

Circle the cause in each sentence.

Draw a line under the effect.

4. I was running with my shoe untied, so I tripped and fell.

5. If you study, then you will be ready for the test.

6. I was hungry because I forgot to eat breakfast.

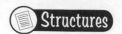

Practice It

Read the passage. Each effect is underlined. Draw a circle around the words that show the cause of each effect.

A Bean Plant Begins

A bean seed will begin to change if it has good soil, water, and sunlight. If you add water to the soil, the roots will grow. Soon the stem and leaves will grow above ground. They will grow toward the sunlight because the sun gives the plant energy.

Answer the questions below.

1. What causes the roots to grow?

_____

2. Why would a plant's stem and leaves grow toward the sunlight?

_____

Apply It

Choose one of the causes in the Cause box on the left and circle it. Fill in the Effect box with a possible effect.

Cause		Effect
• children could vote • there were no televisions	→	

Write a paragraph using the ideas in your graphic organizer.

_____

_____

_____

_____

_____

Learn It

Compare and contrast as you read.

- To **compare** means to ask how things are the same.

- To **contrast** means to ask how things are different.

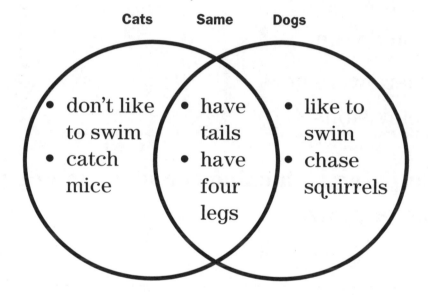

Cats   **Same**   **Dogs**

- don't like to swim
- catch mice

- have tails
- have four legs

- like to swim
- chase squirrels

What is the same about cats and dogs?

   They each have a tail and four legs.

What is different about cats and dogs?

   Cats don't like to swim, but dogs do.

 As you read, ask yourself how things are alike and different.

Try It

Write *compare* for each sentence if it tells how China and the United States are alike. Write *contrast* if it tells how they are different.

1. Both China and the United States are large countries.

   _____

2. China is in Asia, but the United States is in North America.

   _____

3. Mountains and lakes can be found in both the United States and China.

   _____

4. Most people in China speak Mandarin, while most people in the United States speak English.

   _____

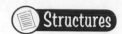

Practice It

Circle the sentences that compare.
Underline the sentences that contrast.

Snakes and Chipmunks

Snakes and chipmunks are both living things. Like chipmunks, snakes breathe air. Both snakes and chipmunks need to eat and drink.

Chipmunks have warm blood, but snakes have cold blood. Unlike snakes, which have scales, chipmunks have fur. Chipmunk babies are born alive, but snakes lay eggs that hatch later.

Use the passage to answer these questions.

1. How are chipmunks and snakes the same?

_____

_____

2. How is the body of a chipmunk different from the body of a snake?

_____

Apply It

Choose one of the pairs of items. Use the Venn diagram to compare and contrast.

- winter/summer
- milk/juice

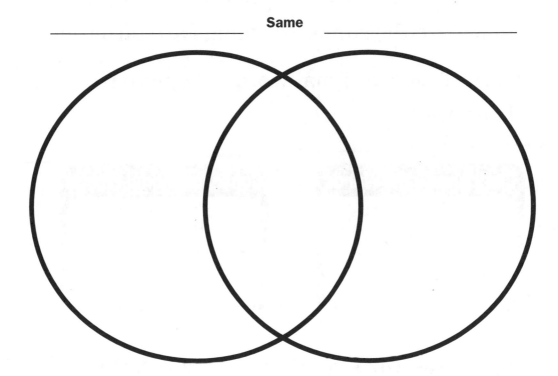

_____   **Same**   _____

Write two to three sentences that tell how the items are the same and different.

_____

_____

_____

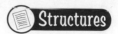

Learn It

When you read, look for ways things are the same and ways they are different.

- To **compare** means to think about how things are the same.

- To **contrast** means to think about how things are different.

Writers often use signal words to compare and contrast.

Compare Signal Words
like
as
same
both

Contrast Signal Words
but
yet
different

 Look for signal words that help you compare and contrast what you read.

Try It

Write *compare* if the sentence tells how baseball and soccer are alike. Write *contrast* if it tells how they are different.

1. Baseball and soccer are both played all over the world.

_____

2. Both games are played on a field.

_____

3. Both games use a ball.

_____

4. Yet, the fields are different.

_____

5. A baseball can fit easily in your hand, but a soccer ball cannot.

_____

6. A baseball has rubber and yarn on the inside, but a soccer ball only has air.

_____

Practice It

Match facts about snow to contrasting facts about rain. The first one is done for you.

Snow

7. Snow is frozen water.

8. It snows in the winter.

9. Snow feels cold.

Rain

Rain feels wet.

Rain is liquid water.

It rains in the spring.

Put the facts above into sentences. Use a signal word in each sentence. Underline the signal word.

10. Snow is frozen water, but rain is liquid water.

11. _____

_____

12. _____

_____

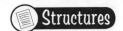

Apply It

Make a T-chart about playing outdoors and playing indoors.

Playing Outdoors	Playing Indoors

Use the information in your T-chart to write a paragraph that compares and contrasts playing outdoors with playing indoors.

_____

_____

_____

_____

Learn It

When you read, look for words that help you make a picture in your mind.

Description words tell what something looks like, sounds like, tastes like, feels like, or smells like. A word web like the one below can help you describe an object.

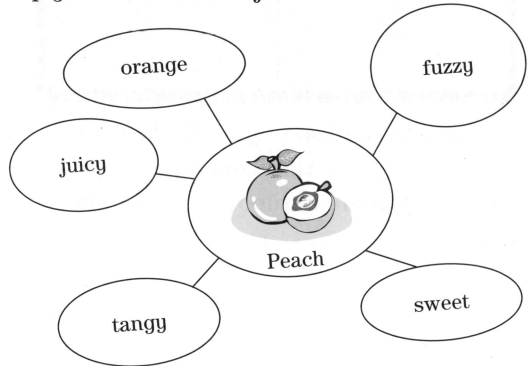

orange

fuzzy

juicy

Peach

tangy

sweet

 As you read, make a picture of what is being described in your mind.

Interactive Skills Handbook • Grade 2

Try It

Read the passage. Circle the describing words. The first one is circled for you.

My Dog, Alma

    I want to tell you about my (yellow) dog. Her name is Alma. She likes to chase red balls. She runs quickly. When we play, she barks loudly. She grabs the smooth, bouncy ball in her mouth. Sometimes she likes to fetch other things. She runs after big sticks that I throw. She even chews on the sticks. I don't think sticks are yummy, but Alma does!

Practice It

**Choose description words from the box to
fill in the missing words in this story.**

happy	younger	red
hard	mad	silly

My _____ brother is a toddler. It
is _____ to understand him when
he babbles. He can get _____. His
face turns _____, and he stomps
around. Sometimes, I make _____
faces to make him smile. When he is
_____, we have fun.

Use the paragraph to fill in the word web.

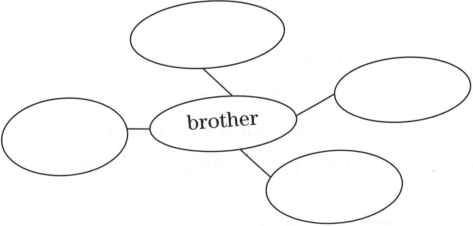

brother

Interactive Skills Handbook • Grade 2

Apply It

Use the web below to describe your breakfast or lunch today.

Write a paragraph about your breakfast or lunch using information from the word web.

_____

_____

_____

_____

Learn It

As you read, look for problems and their solutions.

- A **problem** is something that is wrong.

- A **solution** is how the problem is fixed.

| The grass was getting too tall. | → | Alisha's mother cut the grass with a mower. |

 After you read about a problem, continue to read carefully to understand how it was solved.

Interactive Skills Handbook • Grade 2

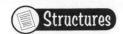

Try It

Match each problem with its solution. The first one has been done for you.

Problem

- My mom says I have to eat my vegetables, but I don't like carrots.

- Kelsey fell asleep in class.

- If I walk to school, I will be late.

Solution

- She decided to go to bed early tonight.

- I will ride my bike to school today.

- I will ask my mom if I can eat broccoli instead.

Write about a problem you had and how you solved it.

Problem: _____

_____

Solution: _____

_____

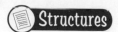

Practice It

Read the letters. Circle the problems.
Underline the solutions.

Dear Advice Lady,

My friend and I fight sometimes. When

he is mad, I try to ignore him. I don't want to

fight anymore. What should I do?

Joey

Dear Joey,

Try talking to him about how you feel. You can

take a break when you become angry.

Advice Lady

Answer these questions.

1. What is Joey and his friend's problem?

_____

2. What solution did the Advice Lady give?

_____

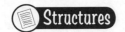

Apply It

Use the graphic organizer to write about a problem that happens at school. In the solution box tell how you can solve it.

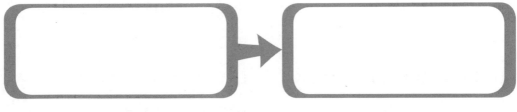

Problem	**Solution**

Use the information from your graphic organizer to fill in the blanks below.

In our school, we have a problem. The problem is _____

_____. We can solve that

problem by _____

_____

_____

_____

_____

Learn It

Problem and Solution

When you read about a problem, look for its solutions.

- A **problem** is something that needs to be fixed.

- The **solution** is the steps taken to fix the problem. There may be more than one solution to a problem.

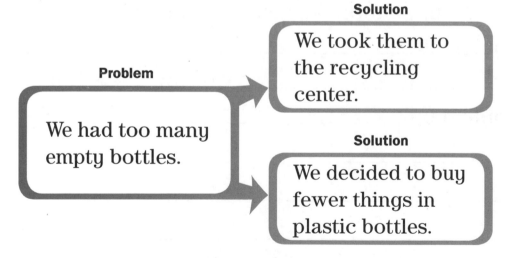

Problem

We had too many empty bottles.

Solution

We took them to the recycling center.

Solution

We decided to buy fewer things in plastic bottles.

 A problem may have more than one solution.

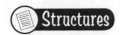

Try It

Fill in the solution to each problem. The first one has been done for you.

- I go to the doctor
- ask a police officer for help
- wait for it to cool before you eat it
- I used a patch to fix it
- ~~everyone helped clean up~~

1. The room was messy, so <u>everyone helped clean up</u>.

2. When I get sick, _____.

3. When your food is too hot, _____ _____.

4. If you are lost, _____ _____.

5. The bike tire was flat, so _____ _____.

Practice It

Read the passage. Underline the problems. Circle the solutions.

> ## Hummingbirds
>
> Getting food can be a problem for birds. Most birds like to eat bugs. But some bugs are hard to catch because they fly very fast. Hummingbirds can fly up, down, sideways, backwards, and upside down to catch bugs. Some birds get food from flowers. This food is hard to reach. Hummingbirds can use their long tongues to get the food.

Answer these questions.

1. How is getting bugs a problem for birds?
   a. Sometimes they are hard to catch.
   b. Birds don't know where to find bugs.

2. How does a hummingbird's body help it catch bugs?
   a. It can sit on top of the bugs.
   b. It can fly in many directions.

Apply It

Think of a problem you have had, such as

- an argument with a friend, or

- a time you had to do something difficult.

Write the problem and two solutions in the graphic organizer below.

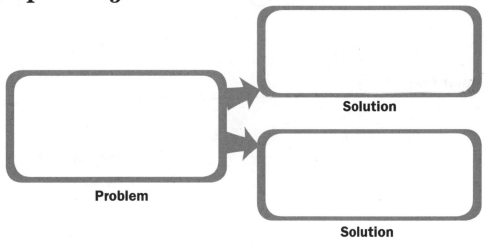

Problem

Solution

Solution

Write a paragraph about the problem and how you solved it.

_____

_____

_____

_____

_____

Structures

Learn It

Sequence is the order of events.

- A **sequence** of events shows the order that things happen.

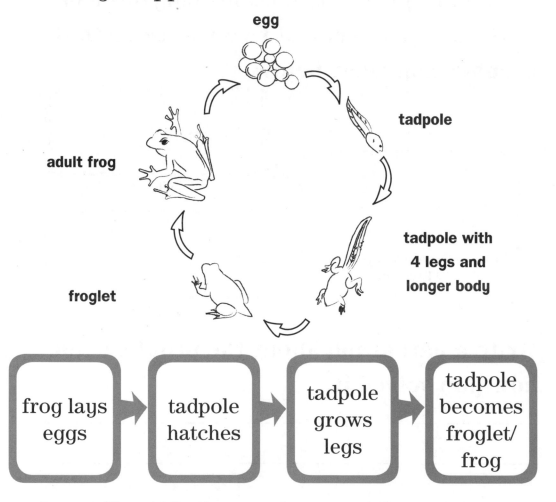

egg

tadpole

tadpole with 4 legs and longer body

froglet

adult frog

| frog lays eggs | → | tadpole hatches | → | tadpole grows legs | → | tadpole becomes froglet/ frog |

 A sequence is the order in which events happen.

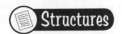

Try It

Write 1, 2, 3, or 4 on each line below to put the steps in the correct sequence.

Movie Munchies

"Movie munchies" are a fun snack you can make and eat while you watch your favorite movie.

How to Make Movie Munchies

_____ Eat and enjoy!

_____ Put the ingredients together in the bowl.

_____ Stir the ingredients with the spoon.

_____ Gather the ingredients: cereal, pretzels, popcorn, raisins, chocolate chips, a large bowl, a cup, and a large spoon.

Practice It

Read the passage below.

Geese on the Move

Every year, geese migrate, or move from one place to another. In the fall, geese leave their homes to move to warmer places in the south. They spend the winter in the warm south. As soon as spring comes and it is warm again, they fly back to their home in the north. Months later, the weather will turn cold. Then the geese will make the long trip again.

Use the passage to complete the graphic organizer. The first step is done for you.

The geese leave the north. → →

Apply It

Write steps for making a sandwich in the graphic organizer.

How to Make a Sandwich

Use the information from the graphic organizer to write directions that tell how to make a sandwich.

_____

_____

_____

_____

_____

_____

Learn It

Sequence is the order of events.

- As you read, pay attention to the sequence. It will help you understand what you read.

- When you see words such as *first*, *next*, and *then* in a sentence, you are reading a sequence of events.

Writers use signal words to show a sequence of events.

Sequence Signal Words				
first	second	third	to begin	now
before	next	then	after that	soon
later	last	until	finally	when

 Sequence signal words will help you understand the order of events.

Try It

Read the passage. Circle the sequence signal words. The first one is circled for you.

The Life of a Plant

(First,) the seed is put in the ground. Next, it is covered with soil. Then, water is added to the soil. After the seed gets enough water, it grows roots and a stem. When the stem grows above the ground, it gets energy from the sun. Water and energy will help the plant grow even bigger. Soon the plant may make a flower. The flower can make new seeds. Later, these seeds can be put in the ground to make a new plant.

Number the sentences 1–3 to tell the order in which things happened.

_____ Roots start to grow.

_____ Water is added to the soil.

_____ The seed is put into the ground.

Practice It

Circle the sequence signal words.

How to Make Bubbles

First, gather soap, sugar, a spoon, and a cup of warm water. Second, add two spoons of soap to the cup of water. Third, add one spoon of sugar. Then stir the mixture very gently for one minute. After stirring, place it in the refrigerator for about five minutes. Last, curl your fingers and dip your hand in the bubble mixture. Now, blow into your curled hand.

Use the steps from the passage to complete the instructions below.

1. Gather soap, sugar, a spoon, and water.

2. Add _____.

3. Add _____.

4. Stir _____.

5. Place _____.

Apply It

Fill in the chart with the steps you take to get ready for school in the morning.

Getting Ready for School

Use the information from the graphic organizer to write a paragraph about how you get ready for school. Make sure to use signal words to show the correct sequence.

_____

_____

_____

_____

_____

_____

Learn It

When you read, think about how what you are reading connects to things you know. **Connecting** means linking what you read to what you know. Connect what you read to

- your own life,
- other books you have read, and
- the outside world.

Mr. Escalante

> Mr. Escalante reminds me of my piano teacher. She taught me to play music that I didn't think I could play.

There was once a teacher named Jamie Escalante. He taught his students how to do very hard math. They passed a very hard test. Mr. Escalante taught the students to work hard and believe in themselves.

 Connecting means linking what you read to what you know. Slow down to make connections as you read.

Try It

Read the story and answer the question.

The Clubhouse

Tony, Ethan, and Sara were building a clubhouse. Tony wanted to use cardboard boxes to build the clubhouse. Ethan wanted to use old sheets and ropes. Sara thought they should use wood because wood is strong.

1. Allen read the story. He thought the children should build a brick clubhouse. His dad told him that bricks are stronger than wood. Allen was connecting to

   a. his own life.

   b. another book he had read.

   c. the outside world.

Practice It

Match each book title with things you can connect it to. The first one is done for you.

Book:

Connects to:

2. *Max Goes Camping*

A. the time your class grew plants

3. *The Big Cats of Africa*

B. *Goldilocks and the Three Bears*

4. *Maria Goes to School*

C. a time your family went camping

5. *Return of the Three Bears*

D. a television show about lions

6. *The Fastest Girl in the World*

E. your first day of school

7. *From Seed to Tree*

F. a news report about Florence Griffith-Joyner, a world record holder for women's track

Apply It

Answer the questions below.

8. If you read a story about the best day of school, how could you connect it to your own life? Write one or two sentences to tell about it.

_____

_____

_____

9. If you read a story about keeping a lion as a pet, how could you connect it to what you know about lions? Write one or two sentences to tell about it.

_____

_____

Learn It

When you read, look for the most important information and ideas.

- The main idea tells what the passage is mostly about. It is often in the first sentence.
- Key details tell more about the main idea.

> The first sentence is the main idea.

The Liberty Bell

The Liberty Bell is a symbol of freedom. In 1776 Americans decided to be free from England. They rang the Liberty Bell to help tell people that they were free. Today the bell still reminds us of freedom.

> The next three sentences tell more about the main idea.

 Rule to Remember **As you read, look for the main idea. Then look for key details that tell more about the main idea.**

Try It

Read the passage below. Find the main idea and key details.

> ### Choosing Healthful Snacks
>
> Healthful foods are good for your body. Fruit and yogurt are healthful foods. Vegetables are good for you too. They have lots of vitamins that will help you grow strong. These foods make tasty, healthful snacks.

1. Which sentence tells the main idea?

    a. Vegetables are good for you too.

    b. Healthful foods are good for your body.

2. Write a sentence that tells a key detail.

    _____

    _____

Practice It

Read the passage below, and answer the question.

The Wright Brothers

Wilbur and Orville Wright wanted to fly. But when they were little, there were no airplanes. One day their father bought them a toy that could fly.

Later, Wilbur and Orville wanted to build a real airplane. They tried many times. At last, they built a real airplane that could fly.

3. Write the main idea and one key detail.

_____

_____

_____

Apply It

Write a paragraph about the most important rule at school. Be sure to include at least two key details that tell why the rule is important. Circle the main idea.

_____

_____

_____

_____

_____

_____

_____

Learn It

Monitoring means checking your understanding as you read. Clarifying means making what you read clear.

As you read, ask yourself questions. Then try to answer them to check your understanding.

> Koalas may look like little gray bears, but they are not. They are more like possums. Koalas come from Australia. They live in tall trees and eat leaves.

These questions might help you check your understanding:

- Is a koala a kind of bear? no

- Where do koalas come from? Australia

 Ask yourself questions to monitor and clarify your understanding as you read.

Try It

Read the passage and complete the chart.

Golden Eagles?

A large bird flies above the playground. It might be a golden eagle. Golden eagles are about 32 inches long. When spread, their wings are about 78 inches across. Their feathers are mostly dark brown. Golden eagles have two lines of light brown feathers on their tails.

Monitoring and Clarifying Questions	Answers From The Text
How big are golden eagles?	
	Golden eagles are mostly brown.

Practice It

Ask yourself monitoring and clarifying questions as you read the passage. Then answer the questions below.

> **The Bill of Rights**
>
> The Bill of Rights is a list of rights that we Americans have. We have freedom of religion or the right to worship as we choose. We have the right to say what we think. We have the right to write what we think. The Bill of Rights lists other rights too.

1. Read the passage again. What does freedom of religion mean?

   _____

   _____

2. Circle the part of the passage that tells what the Bill of Rights is.

3. Underline the rights that Americans have.

Apply It

Read the passage below. Use the table to write questions you may have and the answers you find in the text.

Susan B. Anthony

When Susan B. Anthony was six years old, her teacher said she couldn't learn to do long division because she was a girl. Later, Susan became a teacher. At that time, men made more money than women. Susan worked to change that. She also worked to make sure women could vote.

Monitoring and Clarifying Questions	Answers From The Text

Learn It

Predicting means telling what you think will happen ahead of time.

As you read, use what you know to predict what might happen.

> ### The Balloon
>
> Mom gave Kelly and Marco one balloon each. Marco let go of his balloon. It sailed away. He was sad. Kelly wanted to play with her balloon, but she also wanted Marco to be happy again.

Make a Prediction: What will Kelly do next?

- play with her balloon
- share her balloon with Marco

 Use clues in the story to make predictions and check to see whether your predictions were right.

Try It

Use what you know about making predictions to answer the questions below.

1. Julia is running down the hall with her shoes untied. What do you predict will happen?

   a. Julia will win a gold medal.

   b. Julia will get a "Good Citizen" award.

   c. Julia will trip and fall.

2. Trevor planted a sunflower seed. He put it in the sun and watered it.

   What do you predict will happen?

   a. A tomato plant will grow.

   b. A sunflower plant will grow.

   c. It will rain.

Practice It

Read the passage. Use what you know about predicting to answer the questions.

The Tree Changes

In winter, there are no leaves on the tree. When spring comes, buds begin to form. In the summer, white and pink flowers grow on the tree. In the fall there are shiny, red apples on the tree!

3. Predict what will happen to the tree when spring returns?

_____

Why did you make that prediction?

_____

_____

Apply It

Read the passages in order.

> The alarm went off. The firetruck raced down the street. It pulled up in front of a house, and the firefighters jumped out.

4. What do you predict will happen next?

_____

_____

> The firefighters looked at the house. There was no smoke. The firefighters ran to the backyard. The tree house was on fire. The firefighters got right to work!

5. Was your prediction correct? Why or why not?

_____

_____

Learn It

Asking and answering questions can help you understand what you read.

There are different kinds of questions.

> *What is your favorite kind of weather?* **Answer this question on your own.**

> *What does the weather depend on?* **You have to read the first two sentences to find the answer.**

The Weather

What the weather is like depends on where you live. It also depends on what time of year it is. Sometimes the weather is sunny and bright. Sometimes it is rainy. Rain evaporates and turns into water vapor. When that happens, it may be foggy. When the weather is cold, it may snow. Snow is frozen water vapor.

> *What is it like when it is foggy?* **Use what the writer told you and what you know to answer this question.**

> *What is snow?* **The answer to this question is in the last sentence.**

Where you find the answer depends on the kind of question that was asked.

Try It

Read the passage and answer the questions below.

Letters of Credit

Before there was money, people used to barter, or trade one item for another. Later, people used letters of credit. These letters said a person had money in a bank. They were useful for travel. People could use the letter to get real money so they did not have to carry a lot of money. That way, their money would not get lost or stolen.

1. What does the word *barter* mean?

_____

2. Why were letters of credit better than coins?

_____

_____

Practice It

Read the passage.

The History of Baseball

Baseball started in the United States, but it was based on a game from England called rounders. Rounders was similar to baseball. In the United States, rounders got new rules.

Write the letter that tells where to find the answers. Then write the answers.

a. the answer is right in the text

b. you have to answer on your own

_____ **3.** Where did baseball start?

_____

_____ **4.** Do you like to play baseball? Why or why not?

_____

_____

Apply It

Imagine you are a teacher and you have to write questions about the passage below.

Solar Power

Solar power is a way to use energy from the sun. A special panel catches sunlight. The panel changes the light into electricity. Some gets stored to use later. Solar power costs a lot of money at first. But over time, it saves money.

5. Write a question and the answer that is found in the text.

_____

_____

6. Write a question and the answer that you can answer on your own.

_____

_____

Learn It

Summarizing is retelling the most important parts of what you read.

When you read, ask yourself these questions to help you summarize: Who? What? Where? When? Why? How?

The Sun

The sun is the biggest star in our solar system. It is made of very hot gases that swirl around. Several planets move around the sun, including Earth. Comets and meteors travel quickly around the sun too.

Summary

The sun is the biggest star in our solar system. It is made of gases. Planets, comets, and meteors move around it.

 Summarizing will help you understand what you read.

Try It

Read the passage and answer the questions.

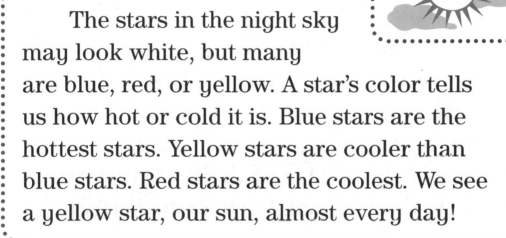

Star Colors

The stars in the night sky may look white, but many are blue, red, or yellow. A star's color tells us how hot or cold it is. Blue stars are the hottest stars. Yellow stars are cooler than blue stars. Red stars are the coolest. We see a yellow star, our sun, almost every day!

1. Which sentence is the best summary?

   a. A star's color tells us how hot or cold it is.

   b. Yellow stars are cooler than red stars.

2. Which sentence is not a good summary?

   a. We see a yellow star almost every day.

   b. A star's color tells us how hot or cold it is.

Practice It

Read the passage and answer the question.

The Perfect Planet

People, plants, and animals can live on Earth because it has water. Earth has plenty of water in its rivers, lakes, and oceans. Other planets do not have much water. Also, the weather on Earth is just right. People could not live on a planet that is too hot or too cold. Earth is the perfect planet for people, plants, and animals.

3. Write a summary of the paragraph.

_____

_____

_____

Apply It

Read the passage, and answer the question.

Robots in Space

    Robots are machines. They do not eat, drink, or get tired like people do. Robots help people do jobs that are not safe. Some robots can go into space.

    Stardust is a robot that was sent into space. It went to an area with no air for people to breathe. Stardust collected small samples in space. It brought them back to Earth.

4. Write a summary for the second paragraph.

_____

_____

_____

Learn It

Visualizing is making a picture in your mind to help you understand what you read.

Use the words to create a picture or a movie in your mind. Use details from the passage.

Homemade Treat

When I walked into the kitchen, I smelled something delicious! It was cold outside, but it was warm inside. My dad was slicing bread that was fresh from the oven. I sat down, and he gave me a piece of the homemade bread. I could see steam rising from it. I put on a pat of butter, and it melted right away. Then I put a spoonful of peach jam on the bread. When I put it in my mouth, it was warm and sweet!

> What would you do if you smelled something delicious?

> What would you be wearing if it were cold outside but warm inside?

> Make a picture in your head of the steam rising and the butter melting.

> How would you react if you tasted this bread?

As you read, use details to help you make a picture in your mind.

Try It

Read the following passage.

A Desert

You are in a desert out west. The sky is blue. The sun is bright. There is no water in sight. You are very hot. You see hills of golden sand. There is a small cactus and some brown rocks. The only animals you have seen are some lizards and a hawk.

Underline three sentences that help you visualize the desert. Use them to help draw what you think the desert would look like.

Practice It

Read the passage and complete the table to visualize what you have read.

Making Maple Syrup

It is fun to see farmers make maple syrup. First, they drill a hole near the bottom of a maple tree. They use little spouts to drain the sap. Clear tree sap slowly drips into a covered bucket. When the bucket fills, the farmers boil the sap over a wood fire. It takes 43 gallons of sap to make one gallon of syrup!

Making Maple Syrup

Looks Like	
Sounds Like	buzzing, dripping, roaring
Tastes Like	
Feels Like	sticky, hot, heavy

Apply It

Choose one of the topics below. Fill out the table with words that help you visualize the topic.

- a day at the beach
- drinking apple cider around a campfire
- playing soccer in the rain

Title: _____

Looks Like	
Sounds Like	
Smells Like	
Tastes Like	
Feels Like	

Use the table above to write a paragraph that helps your reader visualize your topic.

_____

_____

_____

_____

A **sequence chart** shows the order in which something happens.

A **T-chart** compares two things.

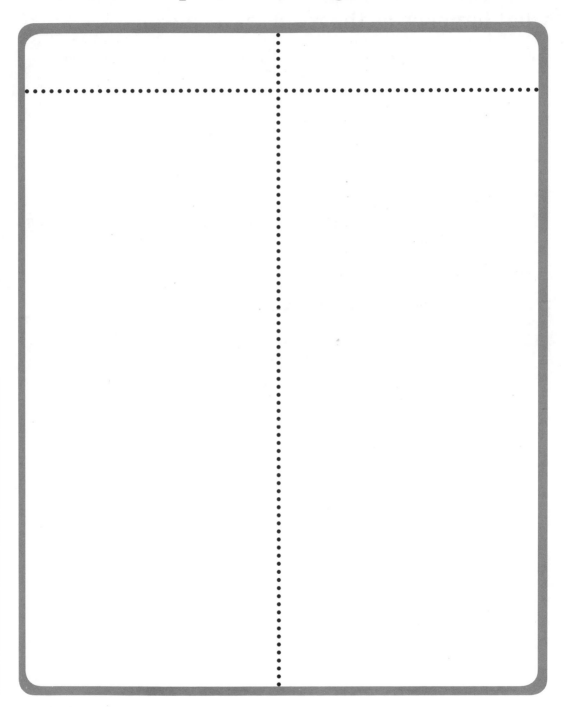

Graphic Organizer — Cause and Effect

A **cause** is why something happens. An **effect** is what happens as the result of a cause.

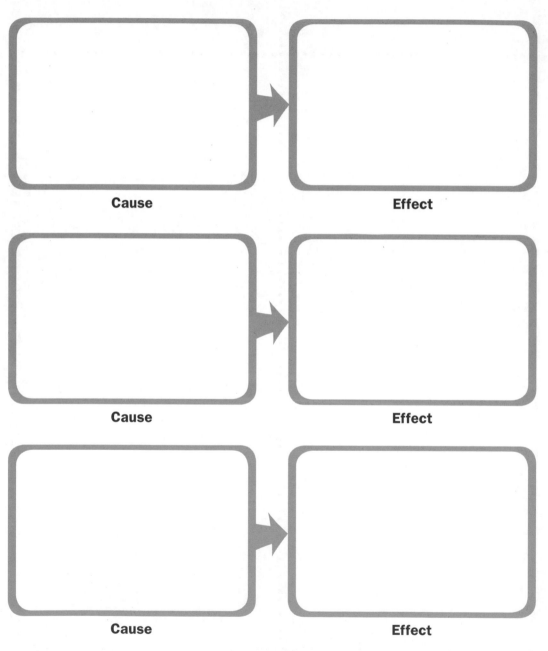

Cause → Effect

Cause → Effect

Cause → Effect

Interactive Skills Handbook • Grade 2

A **problem** is something that needs to be fixed. A **solution** is how a problem gets fixed.

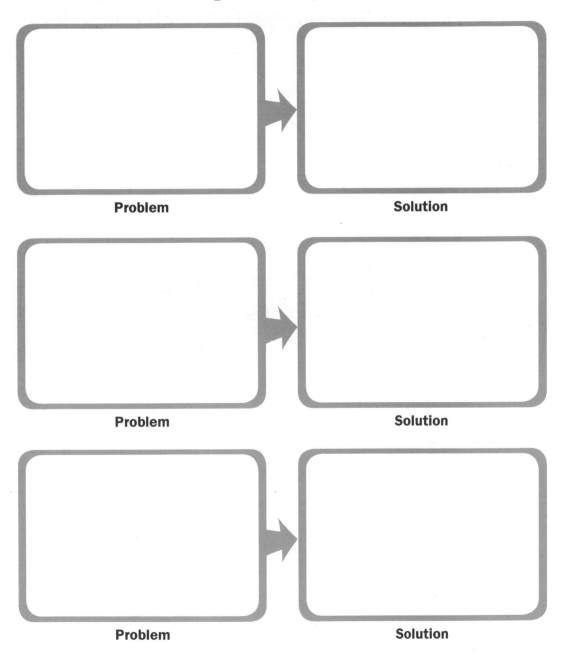

A **Venn diagram** helps you compare and contrast items. To compare is to find out how things are alike. To contrast is to find out how things are different.

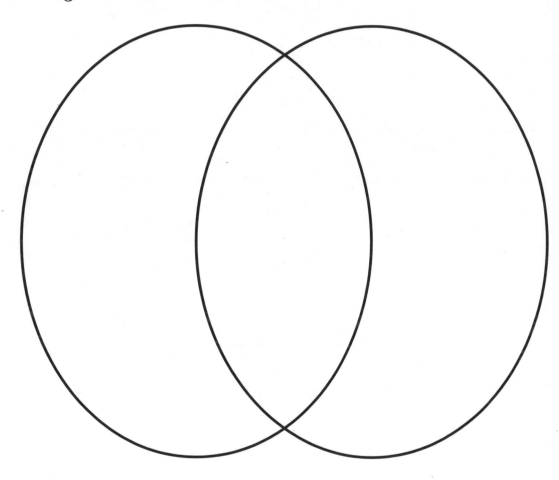

A **web** helps you organize your ideas.

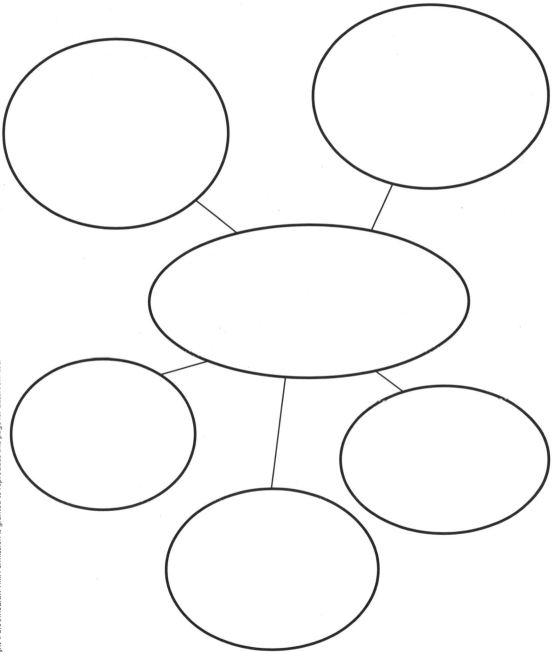